PHOTOGRAPHS BY JUSTIN KERR

LORDS OF THE

MICHAEL D. COE

UNDERWORLD

MASTERPIECES OF
CLASSIC MAYA CERAMICS

THE ART MUSEUM PRINCETON UNIVERSITY

DISTRIBUTED BY
PRINCETON UNIVERSITY PRESS

Dates of the exhibition: March 4–June 18, 1978.

Jacket: Vase in codex style/
palace scene with beheading (see no. 1).
Frontispiece: Detail from polychrome vase/
dancing animal deities (no. 17).

Photographs copyright © 1978 by Justin Kerr,
with the exception of those on the following pages:
17, 23 (Taylor & Dull, Inc.); 29 (Clem Fiori);
35 (Metropolitan Museum of Art); 81 (Jay Whipple);
87, 95, 125 (courtesy of the collectors).

Library of Congress Catalogue Card Number 77-072144
International Standard Book Number 0-691-03917-8

Distributed by Princeton University Press
Princeton, New Jersey 08540
In the United Kingdom
Princeton University Press, Guildford, Surrey

CONTENTS

FOREWORD

The acquisition of a great work of art is a momentous occasion for any museum. Princeton was indeed fortunate to acquire in 1975 the Maya vase in codex style that is the central piece of this exhibition. Number 1 in the catalogue, it takes its place in the Museum's choice collection of pre-Columbian art, a work of rare quality in itself and a touchstone for our future acquisitions.

We owe the vase principally to the generosity of the Hans and Dorothy Widenmann Foundation, and it is cause for sadness that Hans Widenmann, who died in 1976, is not with us to celebrate this first showing of a work that so captured his enthusiasm.

A member of Princeton's class of 1918 and a dedicated alumnus, Hans Widenmann came to this country from Germany as a boy with his parents. He graduated from Princeton with honors, and went on to earn his M.A. and M.Sc. from Columbia. He had a long and successful business career as a stockbroker and economist. At the time of his death he was a limited partner in the brokerage firm of Loeb, Rhoades & Company, of which he had been a partner from 1940 to 1971.

Hans Widenmann traveled extensively and he loved art. His contributions to The Art Museum and to the Library of Princeton University were outstanding. He was a member of the Museum's Advisory Council from 1973 until his death, and his participation at Council meetings was valued by us all, especially by Gillett G. Griffin, Curator of Pre-Columbian Art, and Wen C. Fong, Chairman of the Museum's Executive Committee, who knew him best. Beginning in 1972, Hans Widenmann took a special interest in pre-Columbian gold jewelry and ornaments, and during the next three years he supported the purchase of nine such pieces, all exquisite, which were given to the Museum in memory of his wife, Dorothy, who had died in 1949.

When the Maya vase became available in 1975, it was Professor Fong who suggested to Hans Widenmann that its outstanding quality made it a perfect acquisition for him to support, reflecting his interest in pre-Columbian art as well as his desire to honor the late Mrs. Widenmann's memory. I remember vividly when Hans first viewed the vase; he could not have been more enthusiastic about its acquisition for the Museum and he would tolerate no delay. Thus we were on our way to securing this wonderful work, which has come to be known as the Widenmann vase. I am happy to have the opportunity now to remember this distinguished and generous patron of the Museum. We are grateful too for the support of the Trustees of the Hans and Dorothy Widenmann Foundation, and in particular the Widenmanns' daughter, Elizabeth.

The original owners of the vase, Mildred F. and William Kaplan, not only facilitated its purchase by the Museum, but also presented us with a companion piece, a second vase in the codex style. Our sincerest thanks are extended to the Kaplans, whose generosity has contributed to the continuing growth of our pre-Columbian collection.

The exhibition and this publication have been made possible by a gift from Grace L. Lambert, one of the Museum's most loyal and generous friends. We are indebted to Mrs. Lambert on this occasion, as so often in the past, for her support and encouragement.

Late Classic period of Maya civilization, between A.D. 700 and 800 (Tepeu 2)—the high point of one of the world's great art styles.

The classification system of Maya pottery texts used here is that of Coe 1973. Individual glyphs are numbered according to the Thompson catalogue (Thompson 1962), except where a small x indicates that a glyph cannot be found there; a question mark means that a glyph is illegible or of doubtful identification. Vases given a Grolier number are catalogued in Coe 1973, a Dumbarton Oaks number in Coe 1975, and a Princeton number in the present publication.

INTRODUCTION

There are two ways to view these ceramic masterpieces. The first is in purely visual terms: the colors used, the wonderful Maya "whiplash" line, the beauty of the calligraphy, the graceful movement of arms and limbs, the subtle suggestion of three-dimensional forms on a curved, two-dimensional surface. All of these are worthy of a connoisseur's admiration. But if we confine ourselves to esthetic appreciation alone, we shall be as far off the mark as if we viewed Duccio's *Maestá* in purely formal terms without taking into account the Christian religion. For these lovely vases are imbued with a deeply esoteric meaning which it is the task of the iconographer to reveal. This is not easy, however, since we do not have for the ancient Maya anything like the Bible, the liturgical books, and the hagiographies of the Christian church. Our sources on pre-Conquest Maya thought are fragmentary and often distorted by the myopic bias of the Spanish priests and politicians, whose task was to destroy, not to understand, the alien ways of a conquered people.

In my previous two catalogues (Coe 1973 and Coe 1975), I presented evidence that all Maya pictorial ceramics of the Classic period (A.D. 300–900) were painted and carved for a single purpose: to be placed with the honored dead. They were funerary not only in function but also in iconographic and textual content. The overwhelming majority of the scenes portrayed on Maya vases, bowls, and dishes deal with the Underworld—Xibalbá or "place of fright," as it was known to many of the Maya—and its dread deities. This by no means implies that none of the vases is historical in content. Those that contain the names and titles of real persons, however, seem to refer to them in a posthumous way, recording deeds and honors of the deceased; perhaps they were fashioned on the very eve of the mortuary ceremonies to be put with the dead lord or noble in his last resting place. Such, for instance, is probably the case with Grolier 47, which refers to a high-ranking lady who lived at Naranjo early in the ninth century, or to the battle scene of Grolier 26 and the related ceremonial offering of cloth on Princeton 19. Occasionally these supposedly "historical" vases take up the theme of death by depicting the favorite Maya form of sacrifice—decapitation after torture—or preparations for it.

But it is the Underworld and its dramatis personae that largely claimed the attention of the ancient artists and scribes who made these vessels. It was an incredibly complex realm, with perhaps hundreds of individual deities, each probably associated with a specific disease since sickness, in the Maya view, emanated from their version of Hell. Much of the complexity can be laid to basic Mesoamerican ways of looking at the universe and at the deities who dwelled in it (Nicholson 1971). The universe was stratified, perhaps in Ptolemaic fashion like the layers of an onion, with thirteen layers of heaven and nine of the Underworld; in between was our own world, the earth's surface. Various gods and heavenly bodies had their abodes in specific layers of heaven; and in what the Aztec called the Nine Beyonds there was probably a similar division of function by layer. All three parts of the universe were laid out in the four cardinal directions, each of which was identified with a color and with a World Tree; three other directions—above, center,

and below—formed its central axis. A single great deity, such as the mighty god of the Aztec, Tezcatlipoca, could also exist in quadruple form in the four color directions, each form being iconographically distinct and identifiable.

We know that for the Aztec, who are far and away the best known of all Meso-american cultures, deities—particularly those associated with the central axis—could take on Underworld aspects even if they were mainly identified with the upper world. A noteworthy example is the Sun God, who dies at the end of each day and is taken down into the Underworld by the dread Cihuateteo, female death goddesses of the west, to be reborn at every dawn. The supreme dual divinity of all creation, Ometeotl, who dwells in the thirteenth heaven along the *axis mundi*, has his virtual double in Mictlan-tecuhtli, the lord of the ninth hell.

Another source of complexity, as Nicholson has demonstrated for the Aztec, is the Mesoamerican concept of divinity. Deities tend to fall into what he has termed "complexes," within which motifs and functions of closely related gods or goddesses fade into each other. For instance, there is an important complex of goddesses associated with the moon, sexuality, and ritual pollution, in which the divine figures often interchange head-dresses and other insignia.

And finally, a good many divinities have consorts or lovers. The Aztec Rain God, Tlaloc, is thus not just a four-in-one god: he also has a wife or female companion in Chalchiuhtlicue, Jade Skirt, the patroness of standing water; she in turn is part of a complex including the Goddess of Salt.

To attempt to find order in the multiplicity of deities on Maya vases is no mean task, especially since the ethnohistoric information on the Maya is pitifully slight compared to that for the central Mexicans. But we do have certain leads. First, we sometimes find glyphs associated with the figures, and these can occasionally be identified with gods and glyphs in the surviving Post-Classic codices. Second, I am convinced that certain deities, such as God K, can be linked to Aztec counterparts and thus be better understood.

Most important, we have one great source, the *Popol Vuh*, or Book of Counsel, of the Quiché state in highland Guatemala (Recinos et al. 1950), which contains a detailed description of Xibalbá and its denizens. In the Grolier catalogue (Coe 1973), I was able to demonstrate that the story of the Hero Twins, their descent into the Underworld and their eventual triumph over its rulers, is the subject of a significant number of the scenes depicted on Maya ceramics. On the vases, two aged deities, known to us as Gods L and N for want of their Maya names, are consistently shown as seated on thrones in palaces, receiving the homage of other gods; these must have been the two principal Lords of Xibalbá overcome by the Twins. A pair of youthful divinities, handsomely attired, are depicted as nobles, sometimes dancing in the court of the dread gods; I suggested that these were none other than the Hero Twins, Hunahpu and Xbalanque of the *Popol Vuh*. I see no reason, having now examined hundreds of Maya vases, to change my mind, and I find additional confirmation for this in Princeton 10. But, in the typical Mesoamerican

pattern, the Twins show up in other guises and with other features: for example, in one avatar, which often has them carrying or using blowguns, one is covered with black spots and the other with patches of jaguar skin.

This *Popol Vuh* iconography can be seen in many details of Maya vase painting, such as the frequent depictions on Chamá vases of the Killer Bat, which is responsible for the temporary death of the Twins. These references, often highly metaphorical, are present in some of the pieces pictured in this catalogue. But much of the iconography cannot be explained by anything in the *Popol Vuh,* probably because the Xibalbá episode in that book is only a tiny fragment of a far more extensive chthonic myth or myth cycle that may have been known over the entire Maya area. Thus, we may never have a satisfying explanation of all the macabre and often horrifying tableaux that were carved or painted on clay surfaces.

It is common among Maya archaeologists, not exactly the most imaginative of the anthropological profession, to think of their subject matter in terms of trade, agriculture, class structure, and all the other trappings of modern materialist-determinist scholarship. On the other side, the late Eric Thompson, who certainly did have imagination, conceived of *his* ancient Maya as though they were good High Church Anglicans attending Evensong at King's College. I doubt that either of these two schools of thought would feel at home among the real Maya as shown on a vase like Princeton 20: impersonators of bloodcurdling monsters from the depths of Xibalbá, poised in expectation of the human decapitation they are about to witness, on the verge of a dance to the music of throbbing drums, rattles, and turtle shell, and the doleful sound of wooden trumpets and conch shells. I have always thought that if I were a Mesoamerican captive destined for sacrifice, I would rather have been in the hands of the supposedly bloodthirsty Aztec than in the custody of the "peace-loving" Maya, and I think that these vases bear me out.

In the Grolier catalogue, I also drew attention to the hieroglyphic texts on Maya pictorial ceramics, which had generally been ignored or denigrated by all previous investigators. Far from being illiterate, the ceramic artists were as fully imbued with the practical and mystical aspects of the writing system as the scribes who worked on stone monuments, and in my view their texts were not decorative but meaningful. Particularly interesting is a sequence of glyphs that usually appears in a primary position on a vase, such as in the rim band, which I have termed the Primary Standard text. From this sequence, the artist could select anywhere from a few to over twenty glyphs, but the original text may have contained many times that number of signs. There is still no accepted "translation" of the Primary Standard text, but the Soviet epigrapher Yuri Knorosov and I both believe that it describes the descent into Xibalbá by the Hero Twins and the infernal gods to be encountered there.

If so, then the ultimate function of Maya funerary ceramics becomes clear: they comprise one great mythic cycle, along with explanatory chant, to prepare the defunct for the dread journey into the Underworld, much as the Egyptian Book of the Dead or its

Tibetan counterpart do. Undoubtedly, the complete cycle was once painted on bark-paper codices, the folding-screen books of the Classic Maya that have all disappeared; in fact, evidence will be presented later on that this was so. If it seems unconscionable to us that works of art so incredibly beautiful could have been made only to be buried away from human eyes for all time, that is because we tend to think like Westerners, not like the Maya Indians themselves. For them the honored dead would have seen these works forever.

CATALOGUE

his name might be. It is probably significant that in Post-Classic central Mexican codices such as the Borgia, Mictlantecuhtli, the Lord of Mictlan (the Underworld), is iconographically and functionally the nether representative of Ometeotl, Itzamná's Mexican counterpart.

There must have been a considerable body of mythic literature relating to God L. On the vases and in codices, he lives in a sumptuous palace and has sexual relations with one or more young female deities; he smokes cigars (Grolier 49 and the east jamb of the Temple of the Cross at Palenque); rules over various divinities, including the Jaguar God of the Underworld, the Penis-Perforator Lord, and GI of the Palenque Triad (Grolier 49); and at one point cuts off the head of God K, which he wears as a pendant. However, none of this survives in the extant Maya texts recorded in post-Conquest times.

2

Vase in codex style / throne scene

Collection: The Art Museum, Princeton University, gift of
   Mildred F. and William Kaplan (75-32)
Provenance: Calakmul area, southern Campeche
Height: 12.3 cm
Text: Secondary Nonrepeat
Publication: Coe 1973 (Grolier 43)

As noted in the Grolier catalogue, this vase is supposed to have been found together
with Princeton 1 (Grolier 42), and there are indications that it was carried out by the
same hand. Regrettably, it is in much poorer condition. The scene shows a man and
woman seated on a low throne, facing three other people who make gestures of homage
or carry offerings. I previously concluded that all five persons were deities, and see no
reason to change my mind. The male figure on the throne wears a headdress of a god
who appears to be quite distinctive on Classic Maya pottery: this is a long-lipped deity,
jawless and reptilian, with a recessed forehead marked by turtle-shell crosshatchings and
with a fish nibbling at a waterlily proceeding from this recessed area. The third figure
from the left, immediately facing the lord, is probably identical with one of the canoe
passengers on the incised bones from Tikal: the fourth passenger in both MT 38A and
MT 38C, and the third in MT 51A (Kelley 1976, fig. 80).

The text is as follows, with the Primary Standard sequence extending from A1 to A4:

Primary
Standard
{
A1   61.77:585a (Wing-Quincunx)
A2   x.1000a? (IL-Face?)
A3   78?:513.188 (Muluc)
A4   738.130? (Fish)
}

B   x.x:?

Figure 1
{
C   2?.669b
D   229.501:140
E1   1.539:126 (Half-spotted Ahau)
E2   x.168?:513
}

Figure 2
{
F   x (inverted jar) .606:141
G   832:87
H1   1.539:126 (Half-spotted Ahau)
H2   101?.168?:764 (Calakmul EG)
I   501.528 (Imix-Cauac)
}

Figures
3 and 4
{
J   x.671:140
K   764?.x
L   1.539:126 (Half-spotted Ahau)
M   101?.168?:764 (Calakmul EG)
N   501.528 (Imix-Cauac)
}

As can be seen, the clauses for each figure are somewhat similar. I believe that the name for the Uinal Monster is contained in C and D; for the Waterlily Jaguar in F and G; and for either the shell-blower or the Bearded Dragon, or both, in J and K. It should be noted that the last-named glyphs are also to be found at A1 and A2 of Princeton 5, so that it is probably the Dragon alone that is named. The Half-spotted Ahau glyph would then be a title or epithet of the deity.

4

Vase in codex style / Underworld ritual

Collection: Museum of Primitive Art, New York (MPA 68.7)
Provenance: Calakmul area, southern Campeche
Height: 14.0 cm
Text: Primary Alternative, Secondary Nonrepeat
Publication: Thompson 1970, pl. 14d; Coe 1973 (Grolier 45)

This swirling, dynamic composition involves six Underworld gods in some kind of sacrificial dance. The intended victim is clearly Figure 2, the Jaguar God of the Underworld in infantile form. The executioner is the dancing Figure 1, the deity GI of the Palenque Triad, brandishing an axe in one hand and a head of God C in the other. On the other side dances the skeletal God A, as if waiting to receive the sacrifice. The Jaguar God of the Underworld lies on the enormous head of the Cauac Monster, which often serves as a throne or base in the scenes on pictorial ceramics, and occasionally, in repeated form, as the bottom or side frame to a scene.

Off to the right, Figure 5 is a "jaguarized" dog of sinister appearance, while above hovers Figure 6, an insect that I have previously identified as a firefly holding a cigar. This is an allusion to the incident in the *Popol Vuh* in which the Hero Twins attach fireflies to their cigars in the House of Darkness so as to fool the Lords of Xibalbá.

The text contains the Calendar Round date 7 Muluc 7 Kayab, of possibly astronomical significance.

The role of God GI in the Underworld seems clear: he is a deity of dance and decapitation, as seen not only on this vase but on the polychrome vessel shown as Princeton 8. He is closely associated with the sea, for he has catfish-like barbels around the mouth, wears a shell over the ear, and sometimes has actual fish fins. Why he should be about to execute the Jaguar God of the Underworld is a mystery, for on Grolier 49 the two are seated in God L's palace in such a way as to suggest that the Jaguar God of the Underworld is GI's superior.

6

Vase in codex style / three gods

Collection: anonymous
Provenance: said to be Uaxactun, northern Peten
Height: 28.0 cm
Text: Primary Standard

This masterpiece of Maya ceramic art, taller and narrower than any other vase in the style, was executed by an artist-scribe who was somewhat detached from those responsible for the preceding five vases. The scene was obviously taken from a codex, since the boundary line is drawn as though it were the edge of a page; the more usual method of delineating tableaux was by facing the outermost figures toward the center. The artist of Princeton 6 subverted this canon and by so doing was able to place Figure 1 facing in the "wrong" direction without destroying the integrity of the scene.

Figure 1 is a dancing or prancing personage with a god-eye. He carries a sacrificial axe in one hand and what appears to be an eccentric flint in the other, presumably with the intention of dispatching someone or something offstage. This, along with the short extension of the upper lip, the frontal fang, the bound hair, the pectoral, and the belt, suggests a linkage to GI of the Palenque Triad. However, Figure 1 is virtually identical to Figure 7 of Princeton 12, a helper of GI in a sacrificial role. The only difference between the two is that the loincloth here ends in an animal head, part serpent and part carnivore, emitting smoke from its mouth.

Figure 2 is our friend the Uinal Monster, shown with human torso and limbs like some Egyptian deity. He brandishes a spear directed at Figure 3 in one hand, and a shield seen in profile in the other, while engaged in a dance. The elaborate headdress is decorated with quetzal plumes; to the tied belt of the loincloth are affixed black disks that appear to be obsidian mirrors.

Figure 3 is an aged god with a large god-eye and a Roman nose. He resembles God N and may be a variant on this theme. In place of the netted-element headdress, however, he has a kind of rosette fixed to the front of the hair, seen in three-quarters view, the usual Maya convention for showing a flat, circular object in profile; ribbon-like forms proceed from this rosette. I call this variant God N^1; he is also to be seen on Princeton 7 and 8, and he is probably the God N shown as Figure 2 on Princeton 11. Within the rosette of the headdress of Princeton 6 is T.45, a glyphic element also serving as the prefix for God N in the text. The god here wears a heavy belt like those of the gods on Grolier 49, and he is seated upon a stepped "celestial band." The grackle below the throne adds a unique touch of individuality to this vase; while it obviously serves as a space filler, I have the feeling that it might also be the artist's "signature."

The beautifully drawn text is Primary Standard, but contains some interesting substitutions for well-known main signs:

A	229.x:126 (Initial Sign)		F	25:25.738 (Fish)
B	45.1014a (God N)		G	x (name glyph of Figure 3?)
C	61.77:301 (Wing-Quincunx var.)		H	561:23 (Sky)
D	1000b (IL-Face?)		I	x.116
E	x.88? (probably Perforator God)		J	521:x (Uinal; reference to Figure 2?)

The substitution of a main sign resembling an earspool set for 616–617 in the Initial Sign shows that these elements are interchangeable. A similar interchangeability exists for 585a (Quincunx) and 301 (Footprint) in the Wing-Quincunx compound. This is of real significance, for Landa gives two signs for his letter *b* (or, more properly, the CV syllable *be*): Quincunx and a footprint in a road (*be* in most Mayan languages). 585a is thus to be read as *be* in this context.

Polychrome vase / three gods enthroned

Collection: anonymous
Provenance: unknown, perhaps northern Peten
Height: 23.0 cm
Text: Primary Alternative, Primary Standard

This vase is boldly and strikingly painted, with a rich red background produced by a translucent slip over the lighter base color. The scene depicts enthroned rulers, the principal one being God N[1] (see Princeton 6) seated with his consort, facing another dignitary who occupies a lower and simpler throne.

Figure 1 is a youthful male, quite probably one of the Young Lords since the head of the Jester God worn as a pendant to his necklace is the principal motif associated with this pair of deities in Maya pottery. In the Grolier catalogue (Coe 1973), I have identified the Young Lords with the Hero Twins, a conclusion for which there is further evidence. Figure 1 has a waterlily nose ornament and wears a tie-on "spangled turban," to the front of which is attached the head of a long-lipped god. He holds one of two cylindrical vases, probably filled with drink from the jar behind him. This vessel is shaped like the enema jars used in one of the stranger Underworld rituals (Furst and Coe 1977; see Princeton 11).

Figure 2 is God N[1], also wearing a tie-on "spangled turban," with a rosette fixed to the front; the element within the rosette is repeated as his necklace pendant. He gestures as though receiving the offering before him, a bowl filled with round objects that might be tamales, but that look suspiciously like disembodied death-eyes.

Figure 3 is a young woman wearing a long robe and a waterlily in her hair. The strange device arching up at her back and actually attached to her is T.181, the right half of the sign for the moon. She is therefore none other than the young Moon Goddess, even though she lacks the so-called "lock of hair" that is placed before her face in her appearances in the Dresden Codex. Since this "lock" is most likely the same as Landa's second u (or "moon"), it probably serves as a semantic or phonetic reinforcer in the codices, substituted for by T.181 in this vase. The goddess has various sexual encounters in the Dresden Codex; she is the consort of God L in D.14c, of God A in D.19b, and with two different God Ns in D.21c. A common theme in Jaina figurines consists of an aged deity, probably God N, fondling a young woman who must be the Moon Goddess.

The throne of God N[1] has tau-shaped feet and is embellished on the side with a "celestial band," in this case in the following sequence: Akbal, Kin, Akbal, Lamat-Etz'nab (the sign of the Rabbit God, associated with the moon); the other throne is plain. Below each seems to be a bowl with offerings, but erosion has rendered this hard to make out.

The Primary Standard sequence seems to be present in the rim band, and in the two vertical columns below it.

A	23:x.181		K	77:544.181
B	563a.561b		L	x.565
C	x.x			
D	x.x		M1	1.757
E	542?:713a.181 (Flat-hand Verb?)		M2	563a.501 (Fire-Imix)
F	245.[582]x		M3	168?:552:?
G	1000.181			
H	61.77:585a (Wing-Quincunx)		N1	61.77:585a (Wing-Quincunx)
I	x.23:507		N2	245.1000b?
J	x.526?		N3	109.757:178

In summary, we have a scene familiar in Maya pictorial ceramics, the visit of a Young Lord (or Hero Twin) to the court of one of the Lords of Xibalbá, in this case God N[1].

8 Polychrome vase / ten gods

Collection: anonymous
Provenance: northern Peten
Height: 17.7 cm
Text: Primary Standard, Secondary Nonrepeat

This vase, which is important for its iconography, presents a technicolor view of the Maya hell, Xibalbá. Unusual in the number of colors employed—yellow, orange, red, brown, black, and white—it shows the subtle use of "reverse chiaroscuro," that is, the darkening of inner areas of a rounded surface and the backlighting of outer areas, to give three-dimensionality to the figures. The total effect is superficially cheerful, but actually sinister once the iconography is understood.

This is not one but three scenes, or three acts of a single drama. The scene on the left involves Figures 1 through 4. Dominating the tableau is Figure 4, God GI, with a bound hank of hair, a thorny-oyster shell over his ear, a twisted pectoral, and a loose loincloth belt; he is dancing and at the same time wielding an axe in one hand, a pose familiar on Maya ceramics (see Princeton 4) and depicted on Dumbarton Oaks Relief Panel 2 (Coe and Benson 1966, fig. 6). He has apparently just cut the jaws off Figures 1 and 2, two dwarf-like creatures with deformed, wrinkled heads to which death-eyes are attached; stylized blood streams from their mouths. They are perched on top of a grossly bloated deer, perhaps female as it lacks antlers. Blood trickles down the side of this strange beast.

The central scene comprises only two characters. God N¹ (Figure 6) is seated cross-legged on a throne or bundle covered with a jaguar skin; on the lower half of this is the 667a glyph, which Lounsbury (1973) has demonstrated is to be read *po*, and which in this case stands for rulership. Seated before God N¹ is the anthropomorphic canine divinity with a torn ear (Figure 5). His cheek is marked with a black spot, the sign of death; he must be the dog associated in the Mesoamerican mind with the journey across their version of the River Styx, in which a dog must accompany his master. He reaches up to touch the aged ruler's foot.

On the right is a complex scene involving Figures 7 through 10. To the left, a water bird (Figure 7) is perched on the black head of a jawless Jaguar God of the Underworld, from which sprouts black water-vegetation. This is the well-known chthonic bird, which combines the features of a crane and a cormorant (and perhaps even a pelican at times). Figure 10 is the Headband God with black spots. As in the Blom plate (Blom 1950), where he appears in double form shooting pellets at a fantastic bird with a blowgun, so here he has also shot a bird (Figure 9), the anthropomorphic Vulture God (with the *ti* affix above his beak), who has fallen to the ground at Figure 10's feet.

Identification of the Headband Gods is a puzzle. On some vases, such as Grolier 37, they appear as twins, both with black spots. On others, one has black spots while the other has jaguar-skin patches covering his lower face and god-markings. Of course, one of the distinguishing features of the Hero Twins in the *Popol Vuh* is that they are great blowgunners, and one of their feats is to polish off the bird-monster called 7 Macaw. My own feeling is that the Headband Gods are the same as the Young Lords (i.e., the Hero Twins), but in another role and thus with different characteristics. In this regard, it should be noted that Figure 10 wears the Jester God head, which distinguishes the Young Lords. In fact, my colleague Peter Mathews has suggested to me that the one

with black spots might be Hunahpu, and the other with jaguar markings his twin, Xbalanque (Jaguar-Sun). The Vulture God might therefore be cognate with 7 Macaw.

The Primary Standard text along with other glyphs is found in the rim band, and the Secondary Nonrepeat texts below it:

A	229.616:126 (Initial Sign)		Q4	x.671
B	24:713a.181 (Flat-hand Verb)		Q5	?.?
C	x.88?		Q6	?.?:?
D	1011? (GI)		R	x.617 var. (God K)
E	93?.x		S	x.181
F	x.x.181 (IL-Face?)		T	?
G	61.77:585a (Wing-Quincunx)		U	?
H	x.61:x			
I	323?:x.181		V	x
J	x.x		W	526
K	x.131		X	616b
L	758.110			
M	x.765?		Y	?
N	2?.x.x		Z	?
O	756?.x (Bat?)			
P	x		A'1	1.1030e (present God K)
			A'2	x
Q1	617a var. (God K)		A'3	x:x
Q2	552?		B'1	x.x
Q3	GI? (see D)		B'2	7.x:x

As can be seen, many of the glyphs do not occur in the Thompson catalogue (Thompson 1962). In the Primary Standard text, I suspect that the glyphs from M on contain nominal phrases. The two probable references to God GI should be noted, but elsewhere there seem to be few associations between the glyphs and the scenes; for instance, A'1 through A'3 seem to say nothing about blowgunning, but rather contain a glyph usually connected with the display of the Mannikin Sceptre (God K).

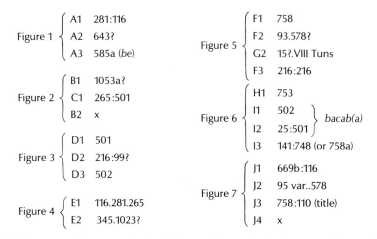

In the case of the two principal figures, the nominal clauses are interesting and significant substitutes for the more usual glyphs. The compound glyph at E2 must be the head form for God L, 1054 in the Dresden Codex; and the "Dog with torn ear" glyph, found at H1, must substitute for God M's usual glyph, 680, since the glyphs that follow are surely titles and/or epithets.

[Not in the exhibition]

10

Chamá polychrome vase / Young Lord and God N

Collection: Duke University Museum of Art, Durham
Provenance: Chamá region, Chixoy River, Guatemala
Height: 14.5 cm
Text: Primary Standard

My contention in the Grolier catalogue (Coe 1973) that the Young Lords represented the Hero Twins of the *Popol Vuh* myth was based in part on a fine Chamá vase (Grolier 16), which shows, as this does, a Young Lord dragging God N from his shell while concealing behind his back the sacrificial knife. The scene recalls the *Popol Vuh* account of how the two rulers of Xibalbá volunteer to be sacrificed by the Hero Twins, expecting—vainly, as it turns out—to be brought to life again following the Twins' own example.

The present vase completely validates my earlier claim. There are, however, interesting differences between the two vases. The knife of Princeton 10, for instance, is hafted in a device resembling the headdress of the Penis Perforator God (Joralemon 1974). To the front of the Young Lord's headdress, which closely resembles the bird-feather dance headdresses of the Indians of San Francisco Bay during the early nineteenth century, is affixed the jawless head of the Jester God, the diagnostic trait of the Young Lords. At the back of his headdress is a Moan-bird feather, a sign of death. His body is painted black, emblematic of death and warfare among the ancient Maya.

God N wears the netted element or bag in his headdress, standing for his Yucatec name, Pauah ("net bag") Tun.

The glyphic text in both the vertical column and in the horizontal row is Primary Standard. However, the glyph at E, Worm-bird, is out of place, belonging more properly between Fire-Imix (at B) and Wing-Quincunx (at C). As I have stated before, this text has no immediate reference to the scene, but must comprise an Underworld litany.

over their respective enemas and jars, while each has his consort behind him engaged in untying his loincloth.

Figure 2 sits crosslegged, wearing a crisscrossed kilt and apparently returning Figure 1's salutation; he has no name glyph of his own in the accompanying text. His headdress is indistinct, but consists of jewels and frontal feathers. Behind him is his consort (Figure 3) in gorgeous robes, her arms tucked under his armpits; her name glyph appears in front of her head, but this may actually be a title since it appears to be shared by two of the other consorts; likewise, her headdress is identical to that of the others.

Figure 4 is the familiar God N of the netted headdress and tie-on turban; to his left is his distinctive name glyph, and the head variant of his name appears as U3 in the text with which he is associated. His consort, Figure 5, is attired and painted like the other robed females, and, like Figure 3, holds her hands in her husband's armpits.

The last two groups are somewhat more complex, since each includes a servant (Figures 6 and 9); these are both attired in wrap-around skirts only, and have God R-like face painting in red. Figure 6 is engaged in fanning her master, Figure 7, an almost naked God N with crewcut hair and open mouth; his glyph is just above his enema jar. Behind him sits his consort, Figure 8, with a turban in one hand which she is obviously about to tie on her husband's head. Below, Figure 9 holds up a mirror to the fourth God N, Figure 10. He in turn is gazing into it and painting his face from a paintpot held in his left hand; his consort, Figure 11, sits stolidly behind him with folded arms.

The import of the scene is clear: these are the preparations for the taking of the enema by the four God Ns. We shall discuss its significance and the identification of God N after examining the long text.

At the top is the Primary Standard sequence, followed by what seems to be a personal name and perhaps a title:

A	229.617a:126 (Initial Sign)	I	513 (Muluc)
B	x:713a (rev.).x	J	507:142.617? (Spotted Kan)
C	1002b	K	181.1000?
D	x (Manik rev.?)	L	61.77:585a (Wing-Quincunx)
E	513 (Muluc)	M	122.1000a?
F	756a (Bat)	N	627:126?.x (Fly Wheel)
G	528.1002a?	O	x.x (personal name?)
H	x (Worm-bird)	P	109.748 ("great ——," title?)

Thompson's so-called Fly Wheel glyph appears in a repetitive band across the extraordinary enema jar illustrated in Furst and Coe (1977), where it is unmistakably an anal sphincter muscle, and my hypothesis would be that 627 is the sign for the enema ritual.

The Secondary Nonrepeat texts within the scene on the vase are extremely important, for they must refer to the deities shown:

Figure 2	Q1	1.x:743:142
	R1	93.x (prob. 672)
	Q2	1000a? (see M)
	R2	109.x ("great ———")
	Q3	126.x:617a inv.?
	R3	x
	Q4	78:513 (Muluc)
	R4	x.116

Figure 3	S1	1002 (female prefix)
	S2	84:501 (Imix)

Figure 4	T1	359?:585a
	U1	Katun
	T2	93.x (see R1)
	U2	561:23 (Sky)
	T3	x.116
	U3	1014a (God N)
	T4	x
	U4	x
	V1	64:x (like 137)
	V2	?:?.582

Figure 5	W1	1002 (female prefix)
	W2	86:528?

Figure 6	X1	1002 (female prefix)
	X2	86:501 (Imix)

Figure 7	Y1	64:281
	Y2	552

Figure 8	Z	1002 (female prefix)

Figures 9 and 10	A'	1002 (female prefix)
	B'	64:713a

Figure 11	C'1	1002 (female prefix)
	C'2	84?:?

Figure 13	D'	1000? (see K)

The outstanding importance of this vase is that it affords an opportunity to examine one of the two great gods of the Maya Underworld in detail. God N is by far the most frequently found deity on Maya pots; this is the god whose glyph occupies the second-most place in the Primary Standard sequence, and it is he who is intimately connected with the enema ritual. I have previously argued that he is identical with Landa's Pauah Tun (Coe 1973, 14–15), a directional divinity. I feel that Thompson's identification of God N and his quadripartite manifestations with the sky-bearing Bacabs is totally in error. In my opinion, the four God Ns stand not on the surface of the earth bearing the sky, but in the Underworld holding up the earth. Information from ceramics, reliefs (e.g., the Temple of the Warriors at Chichen Itza), and the codices suggest that one of these Pauah Tuns lives within a conch shell and bears it upon his back, another within a turtle shell, and a third within a spider web.

In his fourfold manifestation on Princeton 11, one of the figures (Figure 1), has no clear-cut glyphic name; Figure 4 has not only the usual God N designation of 1014a, but also a two-glyph combination which must be read *Pauah Ha* (the 137 sign surely being rain or *ha*). Likewise, Figure 7's principal name must be *Pauah Kan* (reminiscent of Landa's Kan Pauah Tun) and Figure 10's *Pauah* followed by 713a, however that is to be read. Some day the iconography, names, and epithets of this all-important Lord of Xibalbá will be clearer than they now are.

12 Polychrome vase / underwater sacrifice

Collection: anonymous
Provenance: northern Peten or southern Campeche
Height: 22.0 cm
Text: Primary Standard, Secondary Nonrepeat

This delicately drawn vase depicts the ambush of a young god, as he emerges from the open jaws of the Bearded Dragon, by God GI and four lesser divinities related to the latter. That it takes place under water is indicated by the fish attributes of the Bearded Dragon itself (Figure 2), by the fish swimming about, and by the nature of GI (Figure 4), who is correctly thought of as a fish god. The vase should be compared to Dumbarton Oaks 11, in which the Jaguar God of the Underworld and the Perforator God are spearing the Bearded Dragon, which appears with fish attributes in a watery environment.

Figure 2 is the Bearded Dragon, with a bound hank of hair and an upturned snout, crosshatched triangles on a feathered body, and fish tail. This is the creature of the Maya ceremonial bar, often double-headed, and usually emitting the head or head-and-torso of a divinity from the jaws. Figure 3, the young god whose long hair is grasped by Figure 4 in the act of capture, is probably the youthful divinity, or pair of gods, whom I propose to call the Disembodied Head; similar in some respects to the Young Lords, these personages have bell-shaped nose ornaments, often wear jade necklaces, and have swirling face and body paint carried out in red pigment. The reason I call them the Disembodied Head is that many Classic plates and dishes show this divinity only as a head (see Grolier 11); I strongly suspect that what is meant is a severed head, probably of Hun Hunahpu or Vucub Hunahpu, the unfortunate father and uncle of the Hero Twins who lost their lives in the court of the Underworld gods.

The attackers are Figures 1, 4, 5, 6, and 7; all wear brief loincloths and have weapons in hand; all, with the exception of Figure 7, have bound hanks of hair. They comprise the army of Figure 4, God GI of the Palenque Triad. Figure 1 squats on an unknown object and brandishes a feathered spear. His head is much eroded and seems to be in part

repainted, but he must have had a jaguar paw or ear over his ear, and thus is related to the Jaguar God of the Underworld. Figure 4, GI, carries a spear and is dragging Figure 3 from his lair. He wears the typical thorny-oyster shell over the ear and the characteristic pectoral of opposing swirls; a Decorated Ahau can be seen at the back of his bound hair. Between his legs is a fish with the *mo* (582) glyph on the snout, probably referring to his ichthyoid nature.

Figure 5 squats on his haunches, carrying a head or a rock. He might be related to the Maize God, for he wears a stylized maize ear over his own ear, but unlike all representations of that deity in Maya monumental art, he has a large god-eye; if this is the Maize God, it is the only example known to me on Maya ceramics. Figure 6 is a jawless Jaguar God of the Underworld, half-kneeling on the Cauac Monster with spear in hand; typically he has a jaguar paw over his ear, bound hair, and a Decorated Ahau on the head. Figure 7 is identical to Figure 1 on Princeton 6, and the tableaux on both vases are probably related; like that vivacious little god, this fellow brandishes an axe in one hand, and holds what may be an eccentric flint in the other; he half-kneels on an extension of the Cauac Monster.

The Cauac Monster may be seen in Figure 8. The basic freakishness of this deity can be seen in its propensity not only to split and cleave, but also to produce monstrous extensions of itself, such as the malignant growth of a long-lipped head on which Figure 7 perches. Its most important function seems to be to act as a throne or seat for deities and rulers, as can be seen in this vase.

Below the rim band is the Primary Standard sequence plus a number of other glyphs that may have had historical significance:

A	145a?.229.617a (personified) (Initial Sign)	G	747b (Vulture)
B	1000a.181:x (IL-Face)	H	61.77?:585a (Wing-Quincunx, badly restored)
C	88.x	I	?.? (partly restored)
D	738 (Fish)	J	1058?.x
E	582.764?	K	582.x:x
F	501 (personified Imix)	L	109.758a.110 ("great———"; Rodent Bone)

More interesting is the Secondary Nonrepeat text before GI:

M	3 Ik ⎫	P1	V:17:713a (probably name of captive, Figure 3)
N	Seating of Xul ⎬ 3 Ik 0 Xul	P2	x
O	568 pierced:140?.181 (*hulah*, "speared")	P3	738 (Fish, see K; probably name of GI)

The Secondary text thus describes the spearing of the Disembodied Head by God GI on a specific day in the fifty-two-year Calendar Round, underneath the surface of the primordial waters. There is nothing in the surviving Maya mythological records remotely related to this.

14

Red-painted vase / Young Lords dancing with dwarfs

Collection: Marianne Faivre, Dixon, Illinois
Provenance: probably Naranjo, Guatemala
Height: 24.0 cm
Text: Primary Standard, Secondary Nonrepeat

My information indicates that this vase was found together with Grolier 47. The latter bears the name of a woman who is known to have lived at Naranjo, and it has the Emblem Glyph of that site. Accordingly, both of these vases are to be ascribed to Naranjo. In addition, the Vase of the Seven Gods (Grolier 49) has a Primary Standard inscription that is virtually identical to the one here, so that Grolier 49 must also come from Naranjo. There is a number of vases with the same subject of Young Lords dancing with dwarfs, most carried out in various shades of red and orange on a white background, although one in codex style is known. For reasons to be discussed in the description of Princeton 15, Naranjo must be the origin of most of them.

With the exception of Princeton 14, all of these vases depict two Young Lords, richly bedecked, in the act of dancing and occasionally singing. The present vase is unusual and disconcerting because *three* Young Lords are shown, going counter to my usual contention that these must be the Hero Twins of *Popol Vuh* fame. Each dancer is a virtual symphony of iconographic motifs. At the top of the headdress is God K, the lord of royal lineage; at the front is the jawless Jester God, closely related to God K, and that divinity is repeated in the three heads depending from the loincloth belt, which itself is marked by a large thorny-oyster shell. The arms and hands are poised in stylized gestures, and the left leg is raised in a dancing position.

While all three dancers are identical, and thus might be considered triplets, the dwarfs in front of them are all different. Figure 1 is a hunchback with skinny legs and arms, wearing a curlicue headdress; Figure 3 is short and fat, has a clipped shock of hair beneath a stylized thorny-oyster shell ornament on his head, and wears a scalloped shell pectoral; Figure 5 is similar to 3, but lacks a headdress and wears a long necklace.

However, it is the variation of the vertically racked appendages behind each dancer that is most interesting. All three "back-racks" are identical except for the figures seated within them, and share these features:

1) at the top, a bird with God K-like head and serpent-bird wing feathers arching overhead;
2) a "celestial band" with crossed-band segments on which the bird is perched;
3) a deity beneath this, seated and enclosed on three sides, holding a God K head upside down in one hand or paw;
4) the Cauac Monster throne on which the deity is seated;
5) a hanging below the Monster's lower jaw that includes an abbreviated Cauac glyph, a squared god-eye, a complex knot, and quetzal feathers.

The deity with Figure 2 is a quadruped with a Decorated Ahau on the end of the tail and an elongated, upturned snout similar to that of the Bearded Dragon. That with Figure 4 has a semisimian face and holds a brush pen; this is the Monkey-Man God of scribes and artists (Coe 1977). Finally, seated in Figure 6's "back-rack" is the Waterlily Jaguar.

The Primary Standard text from A to M is almost the same as that on Grolier 49, and

J   K   L   M   N   O   P   Q

T1
T2
T3
T4
T5

4   5   6

A   B   C   D   E   F   G   H   I

R1   S1
R2   S2
R3   S3
R4   S4
R5   S5

1   2   3

was certainly carried out by the same hand; the only anomaly is the absence of the jaguar glyph, which is present at M on Grolier 49. The glyphs from N to Q remain a puzzle, P to Q superficially resembling a Distance Number:

N	12.671 [544]:83	P	IV.528:200
O	229.76:x:102	Q	VI.X:501[544].116

It is the Secondary texts that are far more interesting, since they relate to the individual dancing groups:

Figure 2 {
R1	1.757
R2	x.1000a
R3	x.86:561 (Sky)
R4	331.843 (Step)
R5	Calakmul Emblem Glyph

Figure 4 {
S1	1.757
S2	x.1000a
S3	x.86:520 (Chuen)
S4	331.843 (Step)
S5	Machaquilá Emblem Glyph

Figure 6 {
T1	1.757
T2	x.1000a
T3	x.86:524 (Ix)
T4	331.843 (Step)
T5	Tikal Emblem Glyph

There is little doubt in my mind that the repeated combination 1.757 and x.1000a refers to the Young Lords; as another example, one could turn to the Early Classic, stuccoed cylinder from Uaxactun with similar nominal phrases accompanying representations of the enthroned Young Lords (Kelemen 1946, pl. 128a–c). Step (331.843) is taken from the Primary Standard sequence and may stand either for Xibalbá or for the stairs leading down to it. The glyphs that vary are those in the third and fifth places. The final glyphs clearly associate Figure 2 and the skinny hunchback (Figure 1) with Calakmul; Figure 4 and the dwarf with shell pectoral with Machaquilá; and Figure 6 and the fat dwarf wearing a long necklace with Tikal. The glyphs in third place thus apply either to the dwarfs or, as the internal evidence indicates, to the deities in the "back-rack." "Sky" would be the name of the quadruped with upturned snout in the Calakmul scene. "Chuen" is surely Hun Chuen or Ah Chuen, one of the pair of Monkey-Man Gods in the *Popol Vuh* and revered as patron of writing in Late Post-Classic Yucatán; why this deity should be connected with Machaquilá is a mystery, unless that center was noted for its scribes. And finally, Tikal has "Ix," known to be a jaguar hieroglyph, and definitely referring to the Waterlily Jaguar in the "back-rack" of Figure 6. This deity was of great importance at Tikal, perhaps as patron of the royal lineage, and appears as a kind of towering "alter ego" on the lintel from Temple IV.

This vase presents the scene of the Young Lords dancing with dwarfs in its most complete form, no other vase having such clearcut glyphic references to Maya sites. But the general theme is repeated down to tiny details on other examples of the genre. For

instance, a well-known vase reproduced by Gordon and Mason (1925–28, pl. 18) depicts two Young Lords dancing. Accompanying the one on the left is the fat dwarf with the long necklace, and in the dancer's "back-rack" is the Waterlily Jaguar, both characteristic of Tikal; the right-hand figure dances with the skinny hunchback of Calakmul, and while the deity in the "back-rack" is much eroded, it appears to be the quadruped with upturned snout. According to Gann (1918, 138) this vase was found in a burial *chultun* at Yalloch, not far from Naranjo.

Whatever the esoteric significance of these representations may have been, they are important as ritual links between the great Classic centers.

15 Red-painted vase / Young Lords dancing with dwarfs

Collection: anonymous
Provenance: Naranjo, Guatemala
Height: 24.0 cm
Text: Primary Standard, Secondary Nonrepeat

This vase, painted varying shades of red and orange on a white background, should be compared with Princeton 14. While lacking its complexity and richness of text, the dancing groups are obviously largely interchangeable. Figure 1 is the fat dwarf wearing a scalloped shell pectoral who is associated with Machaquilá in Princeton 14, but in place of the Monkey-Man God of that site, there is a mouse-like creature in the "back-rack." Figure 3 is the skinny hunchback of Calakmul, and the same quadruped with upturned snout found on Princeton 14 is to be seen here.

There are a few differences with Princeton 14, none of them of great significance. The seated deities in the "back-racks" hold feathered ornaments rather than the upside-down heads of God K; and an unmistakable God K appears as the head of the bird in Figure 2's "back-rack."

Both Primary and Secondary texts are drawn in a cursory fashion, but are undoubtedly significant. A is the Initial Sign of the Primary Standard sequence, while B is Step. At C is the main element of the Naranjo Emblem Glyph, without the usual affixes.

16

Polychrome vase / enthroned gods

Collection: Walter Randel, New York
Provenance: northern Peten or southern Campeche
Height: 28.0 cm
Text: Primary Repeat

An enormously complex and important tableau of Underworld gods and landscape motifs has been carried out in black, orange, yellow, and resist-produced white on a rich, red background. Although the various deities are unfortunately not accompanied by nominal glyphs, this is a treasure trove for Maya iconographers.

The scene is framed by two gigantic Cauac Monsters (Figures 3 and 10), which perform their usual function as seats or thrones. The central focus is the worship of a World Tree (Figure 6) rising from the head of the Quadripartite Badge God.

Figures 1 and 2 are both deities connected with writing (Coe 1977). The former has a large, bound hank of hair, a feather-like ear extension, and a jaguar-skin kilt; he holds his left hand to the back of Figure 2 and carries a conch-shell paint pot in the other. What makes him unique in Maya funerary ceramics is his character as a kind of "computer print-out": from his armpit proceeds vegetation marked with a series of bar-and-dot numbers, while single digits curl down from his cheek. A very similar "print-out" is to be seen on Itzamná (God D) in Madrid 73b. I would guess that Figure 1 is therefore a patron of mathematics or mathematicians.

Figure 2 has previously been described by me (Coe 1977). This is one of two Monkey-Man Gods of writing, to be identified with Hun Batz and Hun Chuen of the *Popol Vuh*. There is also a connection with the sun, for one of them shows up in the inscriptions as the head and full-figure variant of the Kin sign. Figure 2 carries a codex in the right hand, on which is placed an effigy head, for these scribal gods paint both books and heads.

The Cauac Monster of Figure 3 is very similar to that of Figure 10. However, the Cauac glyph of the former takes on a fish form and the earspool is dotted inside instead of being marked with the Kan Cross. Other heads are affixed to, or grow out of, the original Monster. The one in back is a long-lipped god of some sort; the one attached to the upper lip has a scroll-like nose extension; and the head within the open mouth has a flattened, avian face.

Figure 4 is a wonderfully painted Moan bird looking down on the scene. Attached to the beak is an upturned device with a small black disk, while a larger black disk appears on the tail; could they be mirrors? Extending up from the head is the same motif that is found at the end of the Bearded Dragon's snout.

Our familiar friend God N or Pauah Tun sits to the left side of the World Tree, holding his upraised knee with one hand and bearing in the other an object reminiscent of the pot for facial paint being carried by a God N on Princeton 11. His headdress has the typical netted element, while a kind of speech scroll extends from his upper lip, ending in a flower. This suggests the Aztec metaphor for poetry, *xochicuicatl*, flower-song.

Figure 6, the World Tree, makes up with Figure 7 the central column of the tableau. The vegetation is largely the same as that which emerges on Figure 1's "print-out"; a snake's body winds down it, as in the directional trees in the New Year pages of the Dresden Codex, but the head is lost behind the cartouche of Figure 7. The Quadripartite Badge head from which the tree grows is shown in profile, as on Princeton 13, and is

identified by the crossed bands, an enormous stingray-spine perforator, the thorny-oyster shell, and a Kin sign infixed in the head.

This in turn rests upon Figure 7, which is really a complex of forms and deities. Within a quatrefoil cartouche is a young deity wearing what appears to be a straw hat and gesturing towards God N; only his upper body is shown, beneath a large pair of crossed bands. To the lower left of the cartouche is a goggle-eyed fish, perhaps an indication that the entire scene is taking place underwater; the fact that this water is red need not disturb us, for water is similarly colored on Dumbarton Oaks 11.

It might have been appropriate to consider Figure 9 as part of the complex making up Figure 7. This young female has face painting identical to that on the consorts of the four God Ns of Princeton 11, and it seems safe to assume that she is God N's wife on the present vase. From the evidence of Princeton 7 and various Jaina figurines, I believe that this is also the youthful Moon Goddess.

Figure 10 is another Cauac Monster throne, this time supporting the Jaguar God of the Underworld. The Kan Cross, symbolic of the color yellow in Maya iconography, suggests an association with a color direction. Might there actually be four Cauac Monsters, each associated with a cardinal point? The goateed head attached to the upper lip also differentiates this macabre creature from the Cauac Monster of Figure 3.

The glyphs in the rim band appear to be a kind of Primary Repeat, with Kan (506), Dotted Kan (507), and Muluc (515b) prominent; there is some variation in affixes.

Much of the infernal ceremony on this great vase remains unexplained, such as why these particular deities are engaged in paying homage to a World Tree. And what is the strange object that looks like an Easter egg behind God N? Why is the background divided into red and white areas by a wavy horizontal line?

18 Carved bowl / Principal Bird God

Collection: Barbara and Justin Kerr, New York
Provenance: northern Peten or southern Campeche
Height: 11.0 cm

The Principal Bird God goes back in Maya and proto-Maya iconography to at least Izapan times (Bardawil 1975). Basically, this is a long-lipped god, sometimes anthropomorphic and usually with a reptilian head; he is either winged, or his arms are fitted with wings. These wings, if viewed upside down, are peculiar in that the main structure takes the form of another long-lipped deity, with the feathers spreading out from the upper jaw and lower part of the face like a beard.

That is what is shown here. The head of the Principal Bird God can be seen between the two wings, facing left; its long upper lip reminds one of an elephant's trunk. Irrational though it may seem, the wings are outspread laterally, as though the deity was to be seen frontally but had turned his head to one side. Over the creature's eye is a "down-ball" element very much like one half of Landa's *ma* sign (T.74), and above this a Fly Wheel sign with bone element attached.

Bardawil postulates that the Principal Bird God may possibly be the avian manifestation of Itzamná, the Maya supreme deity, presiding both in the world of the living and the world of the dead. At this point, however, we do not have enough information adequately to explain the Bird's significance. Certainly this was a quadripartite god, since he appears perched on World Trees on Palenque reliefs, and thus should be correlated with the world-direction birds of the central Mexican codices. The Principal Bird God is also very similar to the full-figure forms of the glyphs for Katun and Tun within the Maya Long Count, which suggests that he may have a calendric as well as spatial aspect.

Finally, I should mention the form separating the end feathers of the two wings on this vase. The distortions already apparent in the presentation of the god imply that this is the creature's tail.

19 Polychrome vase in Nebaj style

Collection: anonymous
Provenance: Nebaj, Guatemala highlands
Height: 16.3 cm
Text: Primary Standard, Primary Nonrepeat, Secondary Nonrepeat

This is one of four cylindrical vases in exactly the same style, probably by the same hand, and including some of the same dramatis personae. The other three are: 1) Grolier 26, a vase with a battle scene; 2) the Nebaj Vase, known to be from the same site, with a palace scene (Morley 1946, pl. 89a); and 3) a vase with an even more complex battle scene than Grolier 26 but very similar to it, in a New York private collection.

Before considering the figures in the scene, which obviously takes place in a palace and involves the payment of tribute cloth to a lord, we should examine the text, for it concerns personages here as well as in Grolier 26. In the rim band at the top is the Primary Standard sequence followed by a Primary Nonrepeat text that contains names and titles and/or epithets:

A	229.683b (Initial Sign)		J	12.501:102 (see V1)
B	1014a.x (God N)		K	1.561 (*u-caan*)
C	1.756a (Bat)		L	93?.?
D	501.7 (Imix)		M	1000d?.130
E	62.77:585 (Wing-Quincunx)		N	136.x
F	51.x		O	756 var..116 (Kin-eyed Bat)
G	126.87:513 (Muluc)		P	12.740:181 (Upended Frog, see V2)
H	738.130 (Fish)	in nominal clause,		
I	12.87?:528 (see U)	Figure 4		

A condensed version of the Primary Standard sequence, similar to that on the Nebaj Vase, is found in the prominent vertical column dividing the scene:

Q1	229.683b (Initial Sign)		Q4	501.7 (Imix)
Q2	1014a.x (God N)		Q5	62.77:585 (Wing-Quincunx)
Q3	1.756a (Bat)			

The secondary texts accompanying four of the five figures involved in the scene are of interest, for they connect two and possibly three of the participants with some of the combatants in Grolier 26:

Figure 1
- R1 1.561 (*u-caan*)
- R2 25:534 (*cal*)

Figure 3
- S1 1.561 (*u-caan*)
- T1 25:534 (*cal*)
- S2 582.764:x
- S3 12.126:x
- S4 99

Figure 4
- U 12.87?:528 (see I)
- V1 12.501:102 (see J)
- V2 12.740.181 (see P)

Figure 5
- W1 669b:142.116
- W2 x.x.
- W3 757
- W4 x.130

The scene is dominated by Figure 4, who wears the same headdress complete with tie-on, spangled turban and wraparound waterlilies as Figures 1, 2, and 5; I assume, then,

that the latter belong to Figure 4's retinue. He is seated upon his throne receiving the homage and the offerings of mantles brought by Figure 3, who wears a flamboyant quetzal-plume headdress and carries trophy heads suspended from his belt. On the other side of Figure 4 is the grotesque face of the Jester God, placed in front of a cushion or bundle, and the vertical glyph column of Figure 5.

One would have to illustrate all four Nebaj vases to make complete, or almost complete, sense out of them as regards persons, names, and titles, and that is not my intention in this catalogue. Peter Mathews has suggested to me that the *u-caan* phrase, which I had previously thought to be a title (Coe 1973, 62), is more likely to be the possessive "his captor," and that the battle taking place on Grolier 26 would have happened on a day 2 Akbal within a Katun 7 Ahau. Even so, there are many puzzles to be worked out here, for the nominal glyphs of Figure 3 on Princeton 19 ally him in some way with both Figure 4 and Figure 11 on Grolier 26. Perhaps all three are the same person.

This and its related vases are "historical" in the sense that the figures they depict were obviously actual inhabitants of the Maya highlands. This in no way conflicts with my belief that all Maya pictorial ceramics are related to the dead and to the Underworld, for they were probably commissioned by the man or his survivors to accompany him into the afterlife. This man's name is surely contained in the glyphs found at L and M on Grolier 26, and at N and O here.

20

Polychrome vase / jaguar- and bird-monster impersonators

Collection: anonymous
Provenance: northern Peten, possibly Motul de San José
Height: 19.0 cm
Text: Primary Nonrepeat, Secondary Nonrepeat

This is one of several cylindrical vases in which the human participants in the scene are completely attired in the costume of fantastic animal deities, their own busts appearing in X-ray fashion in a cut-out within the monsters' heads. The actors are heavy and even obese, as are their animal guises, but the outlines are delicate and the delineation of features careful. The mumming of monstrous animals in a ceremony is very much like that in the murals of Room 1, Bonampak, where the performance takes place to the accompaniment of a large orchestra.

Here, the costume of the two principal figures is basically that of a jaguar; but the heads have been grotesquely enlarged and stretched out over what appears to be gigantic deer skulls, with frontal incisors elongated to impossible dimensions. At the back of the jaguar-deer heads are fixed quetzal plumes, making them truly composite beasts. Another, more standardized, jaguar impersonator appears to the right. On the left is a horrific bird impersonator, but the bird is a fantastic one since it has a tail like that of a feline. It should be noted that all four impersonators wear scarves, possibly a badge of sacrifice.

The text is a bit difficult to make out, because of post-deposition alterations to the surface. Perhaps the most significant glyph appears just above the back of the bird monster's head: this is an Emblem Glyph with the main sign of Ik or "wind," which Marcus (1976, fig. 1.9) suggests is associated with Motul de San José, a little-known site in the area of Late Peten Itzá that may have been of considerable importance in the Late Classic period. Since several other "X-ray" vases have this Emblem Glyph, Motul de San José may have been the locus of the style.

C　　　D　　　E　　　F　　　G　　　H　　　I

4　　　　　　　　　　　　　5

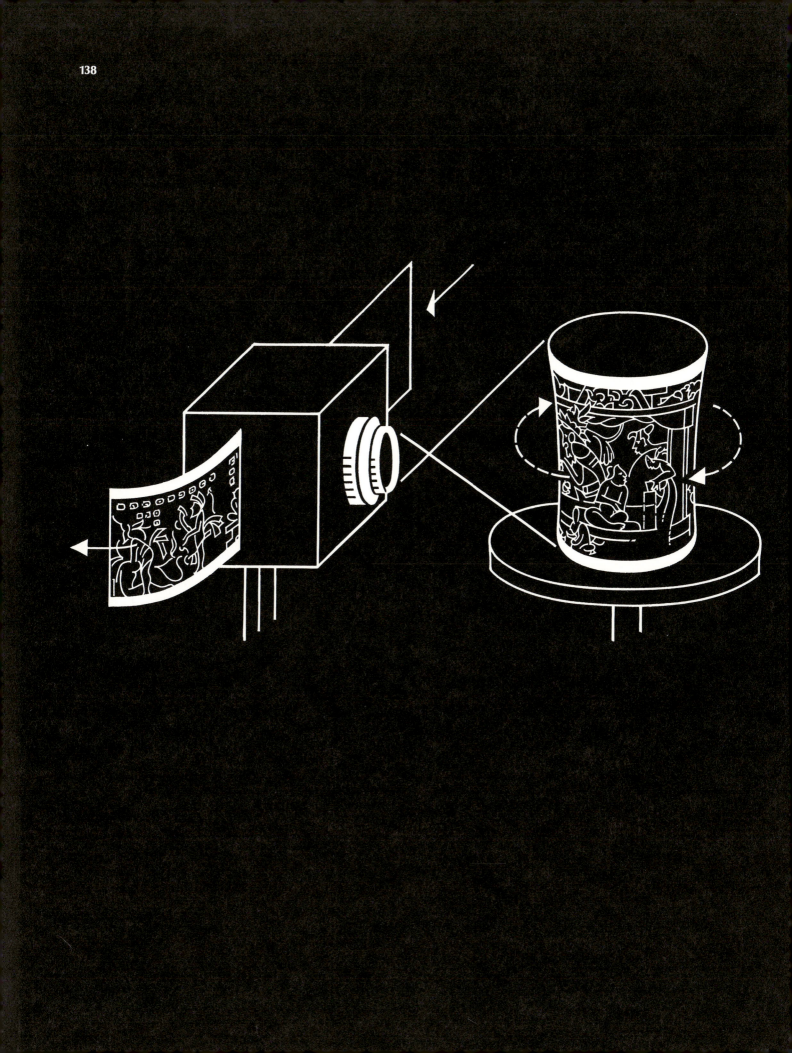

Appendix
THE PHOTOGRAPHIC ROLL-OUT

Some years ago, while photographing a Maya vase now in the collection of Gillett Griffin, I made my first attempt at doing a roll-out, so that the whole design could be seen as a flat picture. I photographed the vase in twelve sections and, with the help of Barbara Kerr, cut the prints into matched, overlapping strips, and then pasted them down to create the "rolled-out" vase. Although this method gave us the appearance of a true re-creation of the design, it distorted the glyphs and figures. It was also very time-consuming and expensive, and difficult to do in color.

I knew then that I would have to find a way to do a photographic roll-out in one step, with as little distortion as possible. I explored many possibilities, and every time the solution seemed near, I would try out the process in my "mind's camera." Invariably, some element of the design would not work owing to the varying contours of the vases.

During this period we did a number of roll-outs by pasting photographs together, but the real solution seemed as far away as ever. In 1973, Michael Coe asked me to do the photographs for *The Maya Scribe and His World*, and we talked about the possibility of making one-step roll-outs for the book. All I had at that time were a few ideas and approaches, but no camera with which to attempt any real work. Finally, in the spring of 1975, with some encouragement from David Joralemon, I started to put the hardware together. I realized that I had been working on the device for almost two years without knowing where all the bits and pieces that I had collected and designed would finally fit. A few days later I had a trial version of the camera ready. The first tests were made of a coffee can, then a perfume bottle, then anything that could turn in front of the camera, and finally, a carved Maya vase. When the film from that first test dripped its way into the light, my hands were shaking with anticipation. When I saw that I actually had the image of a roll-out on the negative, I whooped with joy.

Some months of trial-and-error refinements kept me busy rebuilding and consolidating belts and pulleys, but by the time Gillett Griffin asked me to make the photographs for the Princeton show and catalogue, everything was ready. To explain the process simply: The vase sits on a turntable and revolves in front of the camera, through which the film is moving at the same speed as the surface of the vase (see the diagram). When I look at the camera as it now stands, it is hard to recall the Rube Goldberg devices I had built before arriving at this stage.

In putting the camera together, I have been encouraged by the opportunity it has given me to meet and collaborate with so many wonderful people. I hope to have added a useful tool to the work of decipherment, one that will make it easier for us all to study and appreciate the achievement of these artists. There is personal satisfaction for me in the feeling that I have been able to reach back through the centuries and capture today on film something of the mind and spirit of the great Maya people.

Justin Kerr

BIBLIOGRAPHY

Adams, Richard E. W.

1971 *The Ceramics of Altar de Sacrificios.* Papers of the Peabody Museum, vol. 63, no. 1. Cambridge, Mass.: Peabody Museum of Archaeology and Ethnology, Harvard University.

Bardawil, Lawrence W.

1975 "The Principal Bird Deity in Maya Art—An Iconographic Study of Form and Meaning." In *Segunda Mesa Redonda de Palenque*, edited by M. G. Robertson, pp. 195–210. Pebble Beach, Calif.: Robert Louis Stevenson School, Pre-Columbian Art Research.

Blom, Frans

1950 *A Polychrome Maya Plate from Quintana Roo.* Notes on Middle American Archaeology and Ethnology, no. 98. Cambridge, Mass.: Carnegie Institution of Washington.

Coe, Michael D.

1966 *The Maya.* New York: Frederick W. Praeger.

1973 *The Maya Scribe and His World.* New York: Grolier Club.

1975 *Classic Maya Pottery at Dumbarton Oaks.* Washington, D.C.: Dumbarton Oaks.

1977 "Supernatural Patrons of Maya Scribes and Artists." In *Social Process in Maya Prehistory*, edited by Norman Hammond. New York: Academic Press.

Coe, Michael D., and Benson, Elizabeth P.

1966 *Three Maya Relief Panels at Dumbarton Oaks.* Studies in Pre-Columbian Art and Archaeology, no. 2. Washington, D.C.: Dumbarton Oaks.

Furst, Peter T., and Coe, Michael D.

1977 "Ritual Enemas." *Natural History*, March, vol. 86, no. 3, pp. 88–91.

Gann, Thomas W. F.

1918 *The Maya Indians of Southern Yucatán and Northern British Honduras.* Smithsonian Institution, Bureau of American Ethnology, bull. 64. Washington, D.C.: Government Printing Office.

Gordon, George B., and Mason, J. Alden, eds.

1925–28 *Examples of Maya Pottery in the Museum and Other Collections.* Philadelphia: University Museum, University of Pennsylvania.

Joralemon, David

1974 "Ritual Blood Sacrifice among the Ancient Maya, Part 1." In *Primera Mesa Redonda de Palenque*, part 2, edited by M. G. Robertson, pp. 59–76. Pebble Beach, Calif.: Robert Louis Stevenson School, Pre-Columbian Art Research.

Kelemen, Pál

1946 *Medieval American Art*. 2 vols. New York: Macmillan Co.

Kelley, David H.

1976 *Deciphering the Maya Script*. Austin: University of Texas Press.

Lounsbury, Floyd G.

1973 "On the Derivation and Reading of the 'Ben-Ich' Prefix." In *Mesoamerican Writing Systems*, edited by E. P. Benson, pp. 99–144. Washington, D.C.: Dumbarton Oaks.

Marcus, Joyce

1976 *Emblem and State in the Classic Maya Lowlands*. Washington, D.C.: Dumbarton Oaks.

Morley, Sylvanus G.

1946 *The Ancient Maya*. Stanford, Calif.: Stanford University Press.

Nicholson, Henry B.

1971 "Religion in Pre-Hispanic Central Mexico." In *Handbook of Middle American Indians*, edited by Robert Wauchope, vol. 10, pp. 395–446. Austin: University of Texas Press.

Recinos, Adrian; Goetz, Delia; Morley, Sylvanus G., trans.

1950 *Popul Vuh: The Sacred Book of the Ancient Quiché Maya*. Norman: University of Oklahoma Press.

Robertson, Merle Green

1974 "The Quadripartite Badge—A Badge of Rulership." In *Primera Mesa Redonda de Palenque*, part 1, edited by M. G. Robertson, pp. 77–94. Pebble Beach, Calif.: Robert Louis Stevenson School, Pre-Columbian Art Research.

Thompson, J. Eric S.

1950 *Maya Hieroglyphic Writing: Introduction*. Publication 589. Washington, D.C.: Carnegie Institution of Washington.

1954 *The Rise and Fall of Maya Civilization*. Norman: University of Oklahoma Press.

1962 *A Catalog of Maya Hieroglyphs*. Norman: University of Oklahoma Press.

1970 *Maya History and Religion*. Norman: University of Oklahoma Press.

1973 "Maya Rulers of the Classic Period and the Divine Right of Kings." In *The Iconography of Middle American Sculpture*, by Ignacio Bernal et al., pp. 52–71. New York: Metropolitan Museum of Art.